Boxing Day

Jennifer Howse

Weigl

Published by Weigl Educational Publishers Limited
6325 10th Street SE
Calgary, Alberta
T2H 2Z9

www.weigl.com

Library and Archives Canada Cataloguing in Publication data available upon request.
Fax 403-233-7796 for the attention of the Publishing Records department.

ISBN: 978-1-77071-637-7 (hard cover)
ISBN: 978-1-77071-638-4 (soft cover)

Printed in the United States of America in North Mankato, Minnesota
1 2 3 4 5 6 7 8 9 0 14 13 12 11 10

062010
WEP230610

Editor: Josh Skapin
Design: Terry Paulhus

Weigl acknowledges Getty Images as its primary image supplier for this title.
Library and Archives Canada: page 11.

We gratefully acknowledge the financial support of the Government of Canada through the Canada Book Fund for our
publishing activities.

Contents

What is Boxing Day?

Boxing Day is celebrated on December 26. It is the day after Christmas. Many people have the day off from work and school. They may spend the day ice skating, shopping, or looking at Christmas light displays. Boxing Day is also a time to visit family and friends.

Boxing Day History

The first Boxing Day celebrations began hundreds of years ago. People placed metal boxes outside of churches. Inside each box was an offering to St. Stephen. St. Stephen is a symbol of sacrifice and sharing. He was a saint who helped people in need. The day after Christmas is also known as St. Stephen's Day.

Boxing Day in Great Britain

Great Britain made Boxing Day an official holiday in 1871. At one time, Canada was ruled by Great Britain. Canadians borrowed many traditions, such as Boxing Day, from the British.

Boxing Day Comes to Canada

In 1931, Canadian Prime Minister Richard Bennett made Boxing Day a holiday in Canada. He wanted to give people an extra day off work at Christmastime.

An Official Holiday

In many provinces, Boxing Day is a holiday. This means that people can take the day off from work and still be paid. Most schools are closed as well. If Boxing Day takes place on a weekend, people can take the Monday off instead.

Sporting Events

People often play **outdoor sports** on Boxing Day. Ice hockey is a popular outdoor sport in Canada. Hockey tournaments often take place on Boxing Day. **Team Canada** plays at the World Junior Hockey Championship on Boxing Day.

Shopping Fun

For many people in Canada, Boxing Day is a time to shop. Stores often hold special sales on this day. They sell items at low rates. Some sales that start on Boxing Day last all week.

A Time to Share

A Boxing Day tradition in England is to help people in need. In the 1800s, boxes were kept in churches for people to make donations of money. On December 26, these boxes were opened. The money was given to people in need.

19

Giving Gifts

At one time, people in England would give boxes to their servants on December 26. The boxes were filled with gifts. Servants were also given a day off work to take their box to their family.

A Duke's Deeds

The song "Good King Wenceslas" is about Wenceslas, the Duke of Bohemia. The song says that on St. Stephen's Day, the duke helped a man in need. He gave the man food and supplies to last the rest of the winter. The song is about offering **charity** and doing **good deeds** for others on this day.

Good King Wenceslas

Good King Wenceslas looked out
On the feast of Stephen
When the snow lay round about
Deep and crisp and even
Brightly shone the moon that night
Though the frost was cruel
When a poor man came in sight
Gath'ring winter fuel

"Hither, page, and stand by me
If thou know'st it, telling
Yonder peasant, who is he?
Where and what his dwelling?"
"Sire, he lives a good league hence
Underneath the mountain
Right against the forest fence
By Saint Agnes' fountain."

"Bring me flesh and bring me wine
Bring me pine logs hither
Thou and I will see him dine
When we bear him thither."
Page and monarch forth they went
Forth they went together
Through the rude wind's wild lament
And the bitter weather

"Sire, the night is darker now
And the wind blows stronger
Fails my heart, I know not how,
I can go no longer."
"Mark my footsteps, my good page
Tread thou in them boldly
Thou shalt find the winter's rage
Freeze thy blood less coldly."

In his master's steps he trod
Where the snow lay dinted
Heat was in the very sod
Which the Saint had printed
Therefore, Christian men, be sure
Wealth or rank possessing
Ye who now will bless the poor
Shall yourselves find blessing

Glossary

charity	good deeds
outdoor sports	Team Canada

Index